U.S. Air Force Academy

U.S. Naval Academy

U.S. Military Academy

U.S. Coast Guard Academy

U.S. Merchant Marine Academy

CONTENTS

SECTION 1
DEPARTMENT OF DEFENSE ACADEMIES

3

SECTION 1A
THE NOMINATION AND APPOINTMENT PROCESS

4-8

SECTION 1B
ADMISSIONS PROCEDURES

9

UNITED STATES AIR FORCE ACADEMY

10-13

UNITED STATES NAVAL ACADEMY

14-17

UNITED STATES MILITARY ACADEMY

18-20

SECTION 2
DEPARTMENT OF HOMELAND SECURITY ACADEMY

21

UNITED STATES COAST GUARD ACADEMY

22

SECTION 3
DEPARTMENT OF TRANSPORTATION ACADEMY

23

UNITED STATES MERCHANT MARINE ACADEMY

24-25

SECTION 4
DEPARTMENT OF DEFENSE MEDICAL EXAMINATION REVIEW BOARD (DODMERB)

26

Section 1

DEPARTMENT OF DEFENSE ACADEMIES

AIR FORCE   NAVY   ARMY

SECTION 1A - *The Nomination and Appointment Process*

The Nomination

All appointments to the service academies are made by the President. To be considered for an appointment to a service academy, an applicant must have a nomination from an authorized nominating source. Title 10, U.S. Code, establishes two nomination categories. The first, usually referred to as "congressional nominations," includes the nominations of the Vice President and Members of the United States Senate and House of Representatives. The second, referred to as "service-connected" or "military-affiliated" nominations, includes the selections of the President and nominations of the appropriate service (e.g., Secretary of the Navy for nominations to the Naval Academy).

Applicants should apply to all nomination sources for which they are eligible. Congressional nominations account for approximately three-fourths of all appointments. Therefore, Members of Congress should not exclude from their nomination process those applicants who may also hold service connected nominations.

Congressional Nominations

Members of Congress may nominate applicants who meet the eligibility requirements established by law. Senators nominate from applicants in their entire state. Representatives nominate from applicants domiciled in their congressional districts. Applicants may apply for and receive nominations from both their United States Senators and from their Representative. Applicants may also apply to the Vice President of the United States, who can nominate applicants from the country at large as well as U.S. citizens living abroad.

Service-Affiliated Nominations

An unlimited number of presidential nominations are available for children and legally adopted children of career officer and enlisted personnel of the armed forces, active or reserve, including the Coast Guard. One hundred candidates may be appointed with these nominations each year. A parent in the Reserves must be serving as a member of a reserve component and be credited with at least eight years of service (a minimum total of 2,880 points) or must be entitled to retired pay except that he or she is not yet sixty years old. Otherwise, the parent must currently be on active duty (other than for training) and have served continuously for at least eight years or have retired with pay or have been granted retired or retainer pay. The President may also appoint the children of Medal of Honor winners.

Students may also be appointed to the service academies based on nominations as children of military personnel who were killed in action; died from wounds, injuries or disease while on active duty; sustained 100 percent disability from such wounds, injuries, or disease as certified by the Department of Veterans Affairs; or who are currently prisoners of war (POW) or missing in action (MIA). The children of civilians in POW or MIA status are also eligible. Legally adopted children are eligible.

The Secretary of the appropriate service may nominate for appointment enlisted members of the regular and the reserve components of the appropriate service, members of the service's own Reserve Officer Training Corps and Junior Reserve Officer Training Corps programs, and the Junior Reserve Officer Training programs of the other services which have been designated as Honor Units with Distinction.

Qualified Alternates

If the annual quota of midshipmen/cadets is not filled, the Secretary may select up to 150 candidates who received congressional nominations but were not selected. These candidates must be fully qualified and must be chosen in order of merit.

Additional Appointments

If the annual quota of midshipmen/cadets is still not filled, the Secretary may nominate candidates who competed for the nomination and are fully qualified. At least three-fourths of these candidates must have received a congressional nomination.

Who is Eligible?

Each applicant for a nomination must meet the following eligibility requirements as of 1 July of the year of admission to an academy:

Age: Be at least 17 years old, but not have passed the 23rd birthday.

Citizenship: Must be a U.S. citizen.

Marital Status: Be unmarried, not pregnant, and have no legal obligation to support children or other dependents.

General Admissions Standards

Before nominating an applicant, Members of Congress should carefully evaluate each applicant's overall qualifications, including the legal domicile to confirm that the applicant is domiciled within the state or boundaries of the representative's congressional district. The three academies consider evidence of character, scholarship, leadership, physical aptitude, medical fitness, goals and motivation in determining each nominee's "whole-person" evaluation.

Character

Absolutely critical in the course of evaluating a candidate is a positive determination of the candidate's character. Absence of good moral character is cause for disqualification.

Scholarship

Each element of a candidate's academic record is carefully evaluated by a service academy's admissions board. The elements evaluated include a complete high school record (and college record, when applicable), class rank and either the SAT Reasoning Test scores or the ACT test scores. All strengths and weaknesses in a candidate's academic background are taken into account

SAT scores are available to Members of Congress directly from the testing agency approximately 30 days after an applicant has been tested. However, for Members of Congress to receive them, the applicant must request that the agency forward the test results to the Congressional offices. The applicant may do this at the time he or she registers for the test. It is each Member's responsibility to coordinate with an applicant on the receipt of test scores. Members of Congress may expedite the process by obtaining a SAT code number from the testing agency and providing this code number to applicants. Members may obtain SAT code numbers by calling (609) 771-7600. To obtain ACT test scores, the applicant uses Code 7000 on the test application form. The applicant will then be furnished an additional copy of the test scores to send to his or her Members of Congress.

To register for the SAT Reasoning Test and ACT, students should check with their school counselor or visit the appropriate web site (www.sat.org and www.act.org) for details of test dates and registration requirements. Candidates will normally enhance their competitiveness by taking both the SAT and the ACT more than once. Non-standard, un-timed tests are not acceptable. The admissions offices of the academies stand ready to assist in evaluating test results.

Leadership

Participation and achievement in organized athletics, student body and class government, clubs and class extracurricular activities, scouting, boys/girls state, church or other community-related activities demonstrate evidence of leadership potential. Candidates who have found it necessary to work to provide family support are considered to have demonstrated desirable leadership potential.

Physical Aptitude

Measuring strength, endurance, agility and coordination, the candidate fitness assessment (CFA) is designed to determine each candidate's readiness to undertake the rigorous athletic and physical education program at the academies. Each academy includes the results of the test in their whole-person evaluation.

Motivation

An attempt to measure motivation may be made through observation of the candidate's interest level in attending an academy and serving as an officer in the armed forces. Motivation is an intangible quality and difficult to evaluate; however, since is it most frequently the factor that determines an appointee's success or failure at a service academy, the effort must be made.

Whole-Person Evaluation

All of the preceding factors are part of the "whole-person" evaluation used by each of the academies. These qualities are required of an individual in order to meet the challenges of the academy programs and, following graduation, as commissioned officers.

Applicant Evaluation

Applicants should visit each Academy's website for application instructions.

The applicant must provide the following information: academic standardized test scores (ACT, PSAT, SAT-I), rank in class and grade point average, social security number and participation in high school extracurricular activities. Soon after the applicant submits the questionnaire, the admissions office will reply to the applicant with an evaluation of the applicant's demonstrated ability to meet admissions standards. Applicants who meet the standards are declared candidates; those who do not meet the standards at that point may later submit additional test scores or information to the academy for reevaluation.

Applicant Screening

Status reports for Members of Congress are available online on each academy's congressional website. In addition to considering these candidate status reports, Members are encouraged to conduct their own screening panels as part of the selection process. An alternative is to use a numerical process where numerical weights are given to respective categories of the selection process, e.g. scholarship, athletics, extracurricular activities. A selection committee can assist the staff member in interviewing and screening applicants. The purpose of such a committee is to evaluate, conduct a comparative analysis of, and recommend the best candidates to the Member. The committee should be composed of individuals from different geographic areas and with varied backgrounds including business, education and military service. A Member's staff can make up a screening panel also. To assist the Member efficiently, members of the board should be briefed by a staff member or liaison officer each year as to the requirements of each academy and the latest information in order to make the very best selections possible. To encourage more community involvement, membership on boards or panels should have limited terms.

Vacancies

Each U.S. Senator and Representative may have a maximum of five charged cadets or midshipmen at each service academy at one time. **A Member of Congress may nominate up to ten candidates for each vacancy** (more than one of these nominees may be selected for an appointment, but only one will be recorded as a "charge"). In order not to close out the ability to nominate to each academy each year, **the Member should verify that a vacancy will be available for the next year before filling more than one vacancy.** During the summer, the service academies report who is charged to each office as well as the number of vacancies available for the coming admissions cycle. The Air Force Academy, Naval Academy, and the Military Academy Congressional web pages have real time information on all candidates from a State/District. Status reports are not mailed.

In addition, new Members receive vacancy status reports from each academy shortly after they assume office. For the Air Force and Naval Academies this information is available on the Member's website. Throughout the year, Members are notified by each academy whenever additional vacancies become available because of separations.

Congressional Nomination Methods

There are three methods of nomination which may be used by Members of Congress. They are: competitive, principal with competing alternates, and principal with numbered alternates. Members of Congress may use any of these methods at their discretion. Regardless of the nominating method and means of evaluation used, **it is strongly encouraged that a full slate of ten nominations be submitted for each vacancy**. A higher number of nominees increases the quality of the incoming academy class.

Competitive Nomination

This method of nomination is used by most Members of Congress (approximately 70-75 percent). The Member of Congress submits to an academy an unranked slate of up to ten nominees for each vacancy. The candidates are then ranked in order of merit in accordance with the specific academy's system. The most highly qualified is selected for an offer of admission (an appointment) to fill the vacancy. If the Member has more than one vacancy, ten nominees may be submitted for each vacancy (two vacancies: 20 unranked nominees, three vacancies: 30 nominees, etc.). The academy then selects the best of the qualified nominees to fill each of the available vacancies. **Again, it is strongly encouraged that members nominate as many young men and women as possible for each vacancy, as it enhances the quality of the candidate pool.**

Principal with Competing Alternates

This method provides for designation of a principal nominee by the Member of Congress. The other nine unranked nominees are submitted to the academy for evaluation and compete as alternates. If the principal is fully qualified (character and leadership aptitude, academic potential, medical and physical aptitude), he or she will be appointed and will fill the vacancy. Note that this method does not take into account the quality of the other nominees if the principal nominee is fully qualified. On the other hand, if the principal does not qualify, the alternates then compete for the vacancy. Selection at this point is based on merit as determined by the evaluation and ranking of the alternates by the service academy.

Principal with Numbered Alternates

Under this method, the principal nominee is designated and the alternate nominees are ranked in order of preference by the Member of Congress. If fully qualified, the principal nominee receives the appointment to fill the vacancy. If the principal nominee does not qualify, then the first alternate is

considered for the appointment and so on. In effect, the highest designated nominee who is fully qualified for entrance is appointed to fill the vacancy.

Discussion of Methodology

First: The more competitive the method of selecting and evaluating nominees, the more likely the individual selected for appointment will be the best qualified. In the case of principal nominees designated by Members of Congress, for example, a minimally-qualified designated principal nominee would be offered the Member's appointment, even though one or more of the Member's alternate nominees may be far better qualified. Use of the competitive nomination method ensures that the top-ranked, best-qualified nominee is offered admission.

Second: Use of the competitive method eliminates the requirement for the Member of Congress to rank one constituent over another. Every candidate has an equal chance based on merit and eliminates any perception of political influence.

Appointment of Other Qualified Candidates

In addition to those selected to fill vacancies for a Member of Congress, it is possible that one or more additional nominees of the Member of Congress may be successful in gaining appointments under the qualified alternate or additional appointment categories. These appointments are not charged to the Members of Congress but are charged as qualified alternates and additional appointees.

Early Nominations

There are advantages and disadvantages to making nominations early. **The most significant advantage is that early offers of admission can be extended to outstanding candidates**, thus allowing the service academies to compete with other selective universities for that high quality student. An early admissions decision might be the determining factor that brings an outstanding person to a service academy. Early nomination also provides ample time to replace a withdrawn or disqualified candidate with another nominee, if approved by the specific Academy. Members may submit nominees singularly, or as a partial slate, at any time. This approach is convenient and helps service academies expedite the evaluation of nominees.

It is difficult to advise as to the best deadline date for accepting applications for a nomination. Each Member of Congress has a different volume of applicants, and somewhat different evaluation and selection procedures. **A November deadline date would appear to fit the needs of most congressional offices and still provide for consideration of well-qualified applicants who are late in applying.**

Students are strongly advised to apply to their congressional sponsors and their academy of choice in the spring of their junior year, but many fine prospects do not apply for entry into a service academy until their senior year is well underway and their college plans are being developed. Thus, we encourage Members of Congress to consider substitute nominations as the admissions cycle progresses.

Nomination Deadline

The service academies' administrative deadline for the receipt of nominations is 31 January.

Nominations should be submitted by that time. Late nominations precipitate a last-minute rush to complete admission records. Information is needed from the nominees, their schools and testing agencies. Medical and physical fitness examinations must be scheduled, taken and evaluated. All of this must be completed before an academy completes evaluation of a candidate. In the case of a full slate of ten nominees all competing for the same vacancy, the top individual cannot be selected until all the required records have been received for each of the nominees.

Substitute Nominations

Members of Congress are sometimes asked by a service academy, after their normal process, to nominate a candidate from their district. The appropriate service academy congressional office will contact either the senatorial or congressional district office of the candidate seeking a nomination. Candidates will be used to fill a Member's slate, replace other nominees who decline an offer of appointment, do not apply to the academy, withdraw from the application process, are medically disqualified or whose nomination is withdrawn. The candidates must fulfill all the admissions and congressional office requirements. It is the congressional or senatorial office's decision on approving the substitute nomination. Substitutions may be made by Members after the staffer checks with the appropriate office at the following numbers:

Army (West Point):	**(845) 938-5754**
Navy:	**(410) 293-4392**
Air Force:	**(719) 333-8850**

Submissions of Nominations

The Naval Academy, Air Force Academy and West Point all have online nomination websites. Members of Congress must submit their nominations online via the respective academies web portals. Congressional Staffers are recommended to contact each academy to gain access to the online nomination sites in order to submit their nominations.

Appointment Notification

Candidates to be offered appointments are identified after careful evaluation by each academy. Exceptionally qualified candidates are often offered a letter of assurance (LOA) once they have been found scholastically qualified by the service academy's Admissions Board. The LOA guarantees an offer of appointment after the remaining admissions requirements have been completed. If they have not actually done so, candidates must obtain an official nomination, satisfactorily complete a qualifying medical examination, and pass the candidate fitness assessment (CFA). Each academy may have other specific requirements that must be fulfilled before a fully qualified offer of appointment can be made.

Notification of candidates selected for appointment shall be accomplished by first notifying the nominating sources. The service academies or their congressional liaison offices will notify Congressional Office, so that the Member may contact the appointee.

Publicity

Members of Congress should make wide use of the news media to announce to constituents when applications for nominations to the service academies will be accepted. News releases may be enhanced by information concerning the selection process used by the Member of Congress. An appropriate time for news releases is in the spring when nominations open and again in **September** to announce deadlines for nomination closing. Another release in **January** or **February** is recommended to announce names of all applicants selected for nomination to service academies.

Useful publicity also results from news releases made by Members of Congress concerning noteworthy accomplishments at the service academies by their nominees. Congressional newsletters are also good outlets for these announcements. Local releases, provided periodically to Members of Congress by the service academies, contribute to our common goal of keeping the academies in the public eye and attracting applicants with outstanding qualifications.

Some Members host town meetings which could be an opportunity to bring the advantages of the service academies to a group of potential applicants. Many Members of Congress are now hosting "Academy Days" as another avenue for reaching potential applicants. All academies will render support when possible. Public service announcements by Members of Congress on television programs and communication with local youth groups and school officials are other ways to publicize the service academies as well as the nomination process.

Summary of the Nomination and Appointment Process	
The following schedule may be used as a guide to the timing of important steps in the nomination and appointment process.	
Beginning in the Spring	Members of Congress begin to receive applications for nomination to the service academies. Use news media, newsletters and other means to publicize the application process.
September through December	Members of Congress accept applications and screen applicants, including interview by screening board if used. Members of Congress send out press releases announcing application deadlines.
September through April	Academies provide periodic applicant evaluation to Members of Congress based on the evaluation of the information self-reported by the applicant. In late January or early February, status reports reflect validated information on the candidates. For the Naval Academy, all information is provided online.
Beginning in September	Academies send out early offers of admission/appointment and Letters of Assurance. Advance notice of appointments will be given to congressional offices by the academies. On the Naval Academy Congressional web page, candidates will appear as "Not Evaluated" until the Admissions Board has reviewed the candidate's file, which could be as early as September.
By 31 January (earlier if possible)	Members of Congress submit nominations to each academy.
October through February	Members of Congress send out press releases announcing nominees.
By Late April By 15 April for USNA	Academies have offered the majority of appointments and notified the majority of candidates regarding their final application status.
By 1 May	Candidates must accept or decline their offers of appointment.
May through June	Academies may offer additional appointments to replace candidates who decline their appointments.
Late June or early July	Newly appointed class enters each academy. Members of Congress send out press releases announcing appointees and publicizing the application process.

SECTION 1B – Admissions Procedures

AIR FORCE   NAVY   ARMY

United States Air Force Academy
Colorado Springs, Colorado

United States Air Force Academy
Colorado Springs, Colorado

Academic Requirements

To aid Members of Congress in selecting applicants who have a reasonable chance to compete for an appointment to the Air Force Academy, the following data on college admission test scores is furnished.

The middle 50 percent of candidates with appointments to the Air Force Academy in previous years have had SAT Critical Reading aptitude scores ranging from 590 to 680 and Math aptitude scores ranging from 620 to 710. Comparable ACT scores range from 28 to 33 in English, 28 to 33 in Math, 28 to 33 in Reading and 27 to 33 in Science Reasoning.

Academic preparation and performance are very important. Competitive candidates typically average five college preparatory courses per semester and will complete four years of English, four years of mathematics through pre-calculus or higher, four years of science (to include chemistry with a laboratory), three years of social studies and two years of a foreign language. Many appointees have taken Advanced Placement, International Baccalaureate, or dual enrollment courses.

Medical Requirements

See section 4, Department of Defense Medical Examination Review Board (DODMERB).

Selection Factors

Candidates must rank in the upper 40 percent of their high school class and/or have a satisfactory post-high school record in preparatory school or college, if applicable, but most successful candidates rank in the upper 10 percent.

Academic Composite

The Academic Composite is a combination of the admission test scores (SAT Reasoning Test or ACT) and high school record. Relatively low scores on components of the Academic Composite will often result in an Academic Composite below the qualifying standards.

Candidate Fitness Assessment Score

Each event on the CFA has a qualifying standard and each individual must be able to achieve that standard. Achieving a low score in each event will result in a passing but not necessarily competitive score. Consequently, candidates must perform to the best of their abilities in each event.

Extracurricular Composite Score

Participation in high school extracurricular activities (athletic and non-athletic), or in such activities as scouting, Civil Air Patrol, church, after school employment, etc., make up the Extracurricular Composite Score.

Appointments

Notification of Appointment

Candidates who hold principal nominations will be notified of their appointment as soon as they meet all entrance requirements. All other qualified candidates will be considered for an appointment as soon as their admissions file is complete. Since some appointees may decline their appointment offers, it is possible that some qualified candidates may not be notified of appointment until shortly before the new class enters in late June. Candidates are normally informed in early April that they will not be selected for an appointment. Disqualified candidates may submit additional data until 31 January, such as updated ACT/SAT Reasoning Test scores, a higher rank-in-class or a passing CFA which corrects the noted deficiency(ies). Upon receipt of this information, and if there are no other disqualifying factors, the candidate will be reinstated and notified accordingly. However, until additional data which corrects the deficiency(ies) is received, the candidate will not receive further correspondence from the Admissions office.

Conditional Appointments

Candidates selected for an appointment will be in a conditional status pending determination of their medical status, receipt of college or preparatory school transcript, obtaining U.S. citizenship and successfully completing the Candidate Fitness Assessment (CFA). The conditional offer of appointment will be withdrawn if it is determined that a candidate does not meet the above criteria by their class entry date. Note that all offers of appointment are conditional on continued academic and athletic success as well as exemplary conduct.

Admissions Liaison Officers (ALOs)

Competition among colleges and universities for talented high school graduates is increasing. Therefore, the Air Force Academy places emphasis on assistance at the local level for identifying and counseling qualified young men and women. The Academy looks to the growing number of alumni and to an affiliate Air Force Admissions Liaison Officer (ALO) Program for leadership in field support organizations.

The ALO organization is composed primarily of Air Force Reserve Officers located in all 50 states and some foreign countries. These individuals help identify prospective candidates, encourage them to seek admission to the Academy, and assist candidates actively seeking admission. In addition, they attend "college nights," assist in organizing and escorting educator visits to the Academy, coordinate admissions officer visits to their areas, sponsor cadets on local speaking engagements and support the Cadet Parents' Clubs. When requested to do so, the ALOs may also serve the Members of Congress in whose districts or states they reside on nomination panels. They also provide counseling to students interested in applying for Air Force ROTC scholarships. If you need the name of the ALOs in your area contact the Admissions Office at the Air Force Academy 800-443-9266.

Nominations Office

The Air Force Academy Nominations Office maintains continuous liaison between Members of Congress, the Air Staff and the Air Force Academy regarding candidate nomination, cadet vacancies, appointments and separations. Specific areas of interest to this liaison staff include informing Congressional sponsors of nominees' selections, cadet admissions procedures, and answering Congressional questions on procedures for selecting Academy cadets and Academy Preparatory School students.

The Air Force Academy Nominations Office notifies Congressional sponsors of cadet separations. It determines, in the case of Congressional redistricting, the cadet domiciles, making the necessary Congressional District shifts, and notifying the appropriate Member of Congress of the adjusted cadet quotas. The Nominations Office also organizes the Congressional Staffer visits and escorts the staffers to the Air Force Academy. The Air Force Academy Nominations Office may be reached by calling (719) 333-8850.

USAFA Preparatory School

The U.S. Air Force Academy Preparatory School was established in May 1961. It is located on the USAF Academy grounds about four miles from the cadet area.

The Preparatory School mission is to motivate, prepare, and evaluate selected candidates in an academic, military, moral, and physical environment, to perform successfully and enhance diversity at USAFA. The Preparatory School achieves this mission by qualifying cadet candidates for academy appointments; developing in those students a sense of accomplishment and self-confidence that enables them to succeed in the Academy's demanding environment.

The Preparatory School offers a 10-month program from July through May. The program integrates academic preparation, military training, and athletic conditioning to develop in cadet candidates the skills and character necessary to be successful at the Academy. The primary thrust of the curricula is academic preparation with intensive instruction in Mathematics, English, and Basic Sciences. Course work is fast-paced and challenging.

Like the Air Force Academy, admission to the Preparatory School is competitive with selections made by the Academy Board. The Board selects both enlisted active duty and civilian applicants who have applied for admission to the Academy but were not selected for direct entry. Selection is based on the applicant's high school record, extra-curricular activities, military performance and the results of academic, physical, and medical examinations.

Between 70 and 80 percent of all entering students earn an appointment to the Air Force Academy. To qualify, students must successfully complete the Preparatory School program, pass the Candidate Fitness Assessment, exhibit strong moral character, receive the recommendation of the Preparatory School Commander, and be approved by the Air Force Academy Board.

The Falcon Foundation

The Falcon Foundation, a nonprofit organization headquartered in Colorado Springs, Colorado, assists highly motivated young men and women to qualify and compete for admission to the Air Force Academy through intensive post-high school education at selected civilian preparatory schools. It provides partial scholarships for sponsored candidates. Contact:

> **President, Falcon Foundation**
> **3116 Academy Drive**
> **USAF Academy, CO 80840**
> **Phone (719) 333-4096**

Contact Offices

Selections Division

The Selections Division is responsible for the application and selection process for each new class—from initial application to final presentation of candidates to the Air Force Academy Board for appointment approval. Admissions counselors are available for each candidate to provide assistance on the application process and give them feedback on their status. Additionally, the division oversees the selection panels, and makes recommendations to the Academy Board for appointments. The Selections Division ensures each qualified candidate's application receives a holistic review.

Admissions Liaison and Outreach Division

The Admissions Liaison Division supervises the worldwide United States Air Force Admissions Liaison Officer program which recruits, mentors, and evaluates candidates for Air Force Academy appointments; manages the Air Force Academy Thanksgiving Grass Roots program that coordinates cadet visits to hometown schools and civic organizations; and orchestrates the Air Force Academy Summer Seminar program which brings out rising high school seniors to experience cadet life and attend various academic workshops.

The division also assists in identifying prospective diverse candidates. It provides oversight and is responsible for developing and executing focused recruiting in our Nation's diverse population. Along with the Admissions counselors and ALO force, the division assists the applicants through the admissions process. By organizing recruiting trips, attending college fairs, visiting high schools, and supporting congressional events the division facilitates contact with thousands of potential applicants.

Operations Support Division

The Operations Support Division provides marketing and media, information technology, postal services, and analytical support to the Directorate of Admissions. This division also conducts the daily campus visitation program for prospective candidates and their guests, which annually tours over 2000 candidates and their families.

USAFA Association of Graduates (AOG)

The AOG maintains an office at the Academy to coordinate the activities of graduates. The AOG assists in locating, counseling and motivating candidates through the network of graduates. A number of graduates, both on active duty and reserve status, serve as official Admissions Liaison Officers.

Important Phone Numbers

Director of Admissions	719-333-3070
Academy Nominations Office	719-333-8850
Selections Division	800-443-9266
Admissions Liaison and Outreach Division	719-333-2643
Operations Support Division	719-333-9198
Association of Graduates	719-333-2067

Website: www.academyadmissions.com

13

United States Naval Academy
Annapolis, Maryland

United States Naval Academy
Annapolis, Maryland

Academic Requirements

Evaluating Applicants

In endeavoring to select the best applicants as nominees, Members of Congress should consider the same factors that are considered by the Naval Academy in selecting candidates for appointment.

Factors used to determine the whole-person evaluation include scores on verbal and math portions of the SAT and/or scores on English and math portions of the ACT. The Naval Academy does not consider results of any tests given after the administration of the January SAT Test and/or the administration of the December ACT. For purposes of the admission decision the Naval Academy will use the highest scores achieved on tests taken after December of the student's 11th grade in high school/secondary school. Other factors include the quality of the candidate's academic record (transcripts, class standing and recommendations from school officials) and the extracurricular activities record (accomplishments in athletics, school or class offices held, school and community involvement, the nature and extent of employment during the school year, etc.).

Entering Class Profile

A profile of the latest entering class is provided to each congressional office during the summer. It is also available online at www.usna.edu/Admissions. If you desire additional copies, contact the Naval Academy Nominations and Appointments Office at (410) 293- 4392.

Preliminary Application

Applicants should submit a Preliminary Application to the Naval Academy in the spring of their junior year or as soon thereafter as possible by visiting our website at www.usna.edu/Admissions/and click on 'Apply Now' to start the application process.. This will be used in deciding whether to open a preadmission file. The Naval Academy application is also available on line and can be accessed once a candidate receives their candidate number and specific instructions on the process.

USNA Nominations and Appointments Office

The Nominations and Appointments Office also serves as the USNA's Congressional liaison office. Located at the Academy, it is an integral part of the admissions process.

This office provides a wide range of information to Congressional offices including notice of any midshipmen separations that will affect the number of vacancies available to a Member of Congress. The office is also available to assist with questions on candidates or with information provided on the website.

This office can also provide information regarding all midshipmen currently in the brigade from a specific state or district if requested by the Member of Congress.

Prior to mailing an offer of appointment to a Congressional nominee, this office will call the Congressional Office so that the Member may contact the candidate with the good news. Generally the letter will be mailed 2 or 3 days later.

The Nominations and Appointments office also works with the Department of Defense to select international students and to process the necessary paperwork.

The Naval Academy sponsors an annual Congressional Staff Training Visit in Annapolis, which is designed to help offices identify and nominate competitive candidates. During the visit, participants will see and experience first hand how the 4,000 young men and women of the Brigade of Midshipmen live, study, and train for the very special mission of becoming future leaders of this Nation.

The Nominations and Appointments staff is available to answer questions and concerns that Congressional offices have regarding the nominations process itself, specific candidates, or other issues pertaining to the USNA. Please call 410-293-4392 for assistance.

Vision Requirements

Due to the maritime and aviation environment in which they will eventually serve, candidates who do not have normal color perception must be medically disqualified for admission to the Naval Academy.

The only form of refractive surgery considered for a waiver to enter Navy SEAL and Naval Aviation training is photorefractive keratectomy (PRK). In general, it is prudent to delay all refractive surgery procedures until after the progression of nearsightedness associated with growth in eye size has ceased (beyond age 21 for many people). If a candidate is considering undergoing any refractive surgery or treatment, he/she is strongly encouraged to discuss this with the Senior Medical Officer in Admissions. Refractive surgery is disqualifying and the number of authorized waivers is extremely limited.

Programs Supporting Admissions

Midshipmen as Admissions Representatives

The Naval Academy's Operation Information (OPINFO) Program is conducted primarily during Thanksgiving break. Midshipmen volunteer to make public appearances in their home communities and speak to middle and high school students, appear on radio and television programs, and address civic groups. They provide prospective applicants with invaluable firsthand information on the admissions process and academy life.

Candidate Visits

The Naval Academy Summer Seminar (NASS) is a one week program designed to introduce rising seniors to the Naval Academy. Students will experience all aspects of the Naval Academy including the academic program and midshipman life. Detailed information is available on the USNA website; the application goes on line every year in early January.

Candidate visit weekends are scheduled on specific weekends from September through April for high school juniors and seniors. Candidates must be competitive for an appointment in order to attend and should contact their admissions counselor for more information.

Naval Academy Information (Blue and Gold) Program

This is the Naval Academy's nationwide admissions network. It is headed by the Director of Candidate Guidance at the Naval Academy and coordinated by Navy and Marine Corps officers (admissions officers) at the Naval Academy. There are approximately 2,000 Naval Academy Information Officers (NAIOs) at the heart of the information program, who assist in recruiting efforts throughout the 50 states and overseas. Many NAIOs are Naval and Marine Corps Reserve officers, but there are also a significant number of civilians participating. Many are educators. All are volunteers. It is probable that Members of Congress may already know NAIOs who reside in their state and district. Some are members of congressional nominee screening committees.

Members of Congress are encouraged to call on the NAIOs when they need assistance. The names, addresses and phone numbers of local NAIOs are available from the Nominations and Appointments Office at the Naval Academy.

USNA Alumni Association, Navy League, Midshipmen Parents' Club

In addition to Naval Academy Information Officers, other Navy-oriented organizations located nationwide include local chapters of the Naval Academy Alumni Association and the Navy and Marine Corps League. In some communities, there are organizations composed of parents of midshipmen. These organizations' members, wherever located, are knowledgeable about the Naval Academy. Many would welcome the opportunity to help as a member of a nominee selection committee or in some other way.

The USNA Foundation

The Naval Academy Foundation, headquartered in Annapolis, is a private nonprofit organization chartered under the laws of the state of Maryland for "philanthropic, educational and scientific purposes." The principal mission of the Foundation is to assist highly motivated young men and women to qualify and compete for entrance to the Naval Academy through an intensive year of post-high school education.

The Foundation may provide partial scholarships for those candidates whom it sponsors. A list of the institutions participating is available online at www.usna.com; click on Athletic and Scholarship Programs Division at the bottom of the home page.

Students attending prep school under the sponsorship of the Foundation **must obtain a nomination** in order to receive an appointment to the USNA.

The USNA Preparatory School (NAPS)

Located in Newport, Rhode Island, the primary purpose of NAPS is to prepare enlisted members from the U.S. Navy and Marine Corps to attend and graduate from the Naval Academy as officers. The ten-month course of study, lasting from July through May, is designed to strengthen the academic foundation of individual candidates, with emphasis on English composition, mathematics and science. A student's placement in each subject depends upon his or her demonstrated ability, previous education and additional needs for success at the Naval Academy. Demanding military and physical development programs complement the academic preparation.

Nominees in a regular or reserve Navy or Marine Corps status who are unsuccessful in obtaining an appointment to the Naval Academy are considered automatically by the Naval Academy for admission to NAPS. No special request for this consideration is necessary.

Additionally, each year the Naval Academy Admissions Board identifies a number of the most promising and highly motivated civilian candidates who were unsuccessful in being selected for admission to the Naval Academy. Those identified are offered the opportunity to enlist in the Naval Reserve for the express purpose of attending NAPS.

Candidates for NAPS must:
- be U.S. citizens of good moral character;
- unmarried,
- not pregnant and with no children; and
- at least 17, but not yet 22 on 1 July of the calendar year in which they will enter the preparatory school.

The USNA encourages Members of Congress to nominate students attending NAPS. NAPS students are also eligible for a Secretary of the Navy nomination.

USNA Trident Scholars

Important Phone Numbers

Admissions Office Nominations and Appointments	(410) 293-4392
Associate Director of Athletics Admissions Coordination	(410) 293-2238
U.S. Naval Academy Preparatory School	(410) 841-2692
USNA Foundation	(410) 295-4095
USNA Alumni Association	(410) 295-4000

Website: *www.usna.edu*

United States Military Academy
West Point, New York

United States Military Academy
West Point, New York

Academic Requirements

Members of Congress should consider the same factors as USMA in their selection process for nominations. The USMA Admissions process uses the Whole Candidate Concept which seeks well-rounded candidates who demonstrate excellent academic ability, leadership potential, and overall fitness. Although the Military Academy does not require a specific number of courses or units of study as a prerequisite for admission, recommended areas of preparation are: four years of English, four years of mathematics (including trigonometry), two years of a foreign language, four years of science, (including two years of laboratory science), and one year of history. Overall, a strong college preparatory program taken in high school is highly recommended. Approximately 75 percent of the entering class comes from the top 20 percent of their high school class. Mean SAT Reasoning Test scores for a recent class are Math-654, English-627. Mean ACT scores are Math-29, Verbal-29, Reading-30, Science Reasoning-28.

Congressional Nomination Portal

Each MOC has the ability to track their respective district through the USMA online portal for Congressional Nominations. The objective for congressional offices should be to submit a full slate (ten per vacancy) of eligible nominees to the academy's admissions office NLT 31 Jan each year. Each Member's office can view their respective "Congressional Summary" online at https://nominations.usma.edu/default.cfm. The Congressional Portal allows each MOC office to view Charged Cadets, Nominations submitted for each open vacancy, and Candidates who have started the application process with USMA.

In some cases, a MOC Office may have candidates applying for a nomination who are not listed on the Candidate Summary. This is because the candidate has not opened a file with USMA. The MOC's Office should direct these candidates to the USMA Admissions website to apply online at http://www.westpoint.edu/admissions/SitePages/Home.aspx .

West Point Congressional Liaison Office

The West Point Admissions Congressional Liaison Office maintains liaison with Members of Congress regarding cadet vacancies, candidate nomination, eligibility of nominees, appointment of candidates, and separation of individuals from the Corps of Cadets. The liaison office informs Congressional sponsors of the nominees' selection two days prior to the announcement by the admissions office. Each August, the office also informs Members of Congress of the number of cadet vacancies they will have for the next entering class.

The West Point Admissions Congressional Liaison Office determines, in the case of redistricting, the congressional district to which affected cadets and candidates are chargeable according to domicile. The liaison office also notifies appropriate Congressional sponsors of all cadet separations.

This office, through its work with the State Department, maintains up-to-date information on the number of foreign cadet vacancies at the Military Academy. The West Point Admissions Congressional Liaison Office may be reached by calling (845) 938-5754/5723, or by writing:

Director of Admissions
ATTN: Congressional Liaison
Building 606
West Point, New York
10996-1905

Spheres of Influence/Service Academy Day Events

USMA looks to its alumni and affiliated organizations (West Point Parents Clubs, West Point Societies) for support of its community oriented recruitment and outreach programs. USMA's Spheres of Influence consist of its Outreach Officers, grads, parents, and community leaders to help identify and encourage candidates to apply. Our Outreach Office, Field Force members, and Military Academy Liaison Officers (MALOs) can help develop programs or events that might help shape and ultimately increase the potential candidate pool in a MOC's respective district.

Field force members make up the majority of our volunteer Admissions support team. They serve as State Coordinators, Congressional District Coordinators, or local representatives in your area. Individuals in Field Force roles identify prospective candidates, encourage them to apply, advise and assist candidates throughout the nomination and application processes. The Military Academy Liaison Officer (MALO) program is another admissions group operating at the local level. The MALO, a U.S. Army Reserve Officer, performs admissions counseling and recruiting tasks within and assigned area.

Service Academy Day events are great opportunities for MOCs to inform and inspire their constituents to serve. USMA Admissions Officers and field support personnel attend Academy Day events sponsored by MOC Offices. Academy Days are a gateway into garnering Service Academy interest within a Congressional District. These events are highly encouraged for all Members of Congress to consider. USMA can support these events with current cadets from your State or District if requested by the Congressional Staff. A request should be made at least one month in advance.

Candidate Orientation Visits

West Point sponsors daily candidate orientation visits for high school students and their families Monday through Friday during the academic year (Sep-Apr). Candidates that have received a Letter of Assurance, Letter of Encouragement or Offer of Admission are eligible for an overnight visit. All visits are by appointment only during the Academic Year. Summer visits (May-Aug) do not require an appointment, but visitors are encouraged to call ahead of time to ensure a date is available to attend the daily brief. Candidates interested in visiting West Point should call 845-938-5759/5760 to arrange a visit or visit the West Point Admissions website at http://www.westpoint.edu/admissions/SitePages/Visit.aspx.

Outreach Recruiting Programs

The admissions office continues to identify, encourage and assist Outreach candidates who are interested in gaining admission to West Point. Our Outreach Office utilizes a team of Officers that visit the homes of academically promising students to promote the academy and present firsthand accounts of academy life. They also speak at high schools, college fairs, and civic groups to advise, assist and inform local communities about USMA and the opportunities it presents.

USMA Preparatory School (USMAPS)

The United States Military Academy Preparatory School (USMAPS) at West Point, NY, prepares candidates selected by the USMA Admissions office for the academic, physical, and military challenges of USMA. Every year the Admissions Office can select up to 246 candidates to attend USMAPS. Approximately 80-85% of every graduating USMAPS class gains an offer of admission to USMA. An applicant for USMAPS must meet the basic requirements for nomination to the Military Academy or have already received a nomination. USMAPS emphasizes instruction in Mathematics, English, and Student Development Courses. Detailed information about USMAPS can be found at http://www.usma.edu/usmaps/SitePages/Home.aspx or by contacting the Soldiers Admissions Officer at 845-938-5780.

Cadet Hometown Visits

Every year, approximately 500 West Point cadets make public appearances before school audiences, civic organizations and on radio and TV programs in support of our Hometown Visitation Program. Cadets are some of the most effective admissions and public relations representatives for West Point. Cadets make their appearances in conjunction with Thanksgiving leave and Spring Break (March). During the academic year cadets also participate in Service Academy Days, by-invitation meetings and college fairs across the country. Contact the Congressional Liaison Office at 845-938-5754/5723 to request cadet speakers more than one month in advance.

West Point Preparatory Scholarship Program

The West Point Preparatory Scholarship Program (WPPSP) was established in 1979 in conjunction with the Director of Admissions, USMA. The program is designed to provide partial scholarships for a year of post secondary school education at preparatory schools and military junior colleges for carefully selected and highly motivated young people seeking admission to the United States Military Academy. The West Point Preparatory Scholarship Program supplements the United States Military Academy Preparatory School (USMAPS), and provides a broader-based preparation than USMAPS. While USMAPS teaches only Math, English, and the SAT, the WPPSP requires candidates to take a full course load. The WPPSP offers an alternative path to West Point for candidates who do not need the specialized preparation provided by USMAPS, but can benefit from an additional year of academics.

Important Phone Numbers

Directorate of Admissions (including Regional Admissions Officers and Minority Recruiting): (845) 938-4041
Website:
http://www.westpoint.edu/admissions/SitePages/Home.aspx
.

SECTION 2

Department of Homeland Security Academy

U.S. Coast Guard Academy

United States Coast Guard Academy
New London, Connecticut

Admissions Information

Requirements

The U.S. Coast Guard Academy (CGA) is the only one of the armed forces service academies that offers appointments solely on the basis of a nationwide merit-based competition; there are no congressional nominations or geographic quotas involved. Applicants must be U.S. citizens between 17 and 22 years old upon entering the academy. They must meet basic eligibility requirements and undergo a holistic application review including consideration of SAT Reasoning Test or American College Testing (ACT) Program examination results, high school standing and leadership potential as demonstrated by participation in extracurricular activities and community affairs or part-time employment. Most successful candidates graduate in the top quarter of their high school class and demonstrate proficiency in both the mathematical and applied science fields. Either the ACT with Writing Test or SAT Reasoning Test must be completed prior to or during the January test administration of the year of entry.

Application

Applicants can access the on-line application directly at www.uscga.edu/apply. A non-binding Early Action program is available for students who complete their application and submit all required application items by October 15th; the final admissions deadline is January 15th. Applicants must submit the on-line application, an official high school transcript, official standardized test scores, a letter of recommendation from a school counselor, letters of recommendation from an English and mathematics teacher, and complete a standard Physical Fitness Examination to be eligible for review. Additionally, to receive an appointment, applicants must complete a medical examination and be found qualified by the Department of Defense Medical Examination Review Board.

Field Support/Introductory Programs

A network of over 800 Academy Admissions Partners plays an important role in recruiting and assisting prospective cadets. Academy Admissions Partners are made up of alumni, CG active duty and reservists, as well as Auxiliarists and parents of cadets.

The Coast Guard Academy conducts a one-week summer program for students between their junior and senior year of high school. The Academy Introduction Mission (AIM) Program is is run by the CGA Admissions Division with support from Admissions Partners and engineering faculty; 2/c [junior] cadets act as mentors and supervisors for all attendees. Students who participate in AIM are exposed to cadet life, given tours of operational Coast Guard assets, and complete an engineering project sponsored by the Accreditation Board for Engineering and Technology (ABET). Applications are available on the academy's website from early February through early April. Additional information about the AIM program can be found on the academy's website www.uscga.edu/AIM.

Preparatory Programs

The Coast Guard Academy Scholars (CGAS) Program is a ten-month program of study in mathematics, physics, chemistry, English, athletic and military training designed to fully prepare Cadet Candidates for the rigorous program at the Academy.

Cadet Candidates are selected from the overall CGA applicant pool, based on the Cadet Candidates Evaluation Board's determination for their propensity to succeed at the Academy after one year of preparation. They arrive at CGA during the summer before reporting to their prep schools for three weeks of basic indoctrination and accession as an active duty enlisted member.

After the three week orientation, Cadet Candidates will be assigned to one of two private military institutions the Academy utilizes; either Marion Military Institute (in Marion, Alabama) or Georgia Military College (in Milledgeville, Georgia). Following successful completion of the program, students will report to the Academy to begin the four year program as cadets.

Important Phone Numbers

Director of Admissions	(860) 444-8500
Assoc Director for Operations	(860) 701-6778
Assoc Director for Recruiting	(860) 701-6783
Toll Free (Automated System)	(800) 883-8724

Website: www.uscga.edu

SECTION 3

Department of Transportation Academy

U.S. Merchant Marine Academy

United States Merchant Marine Academy
Kings Point, New York

The United States Merchant Marine Academy (USMMA), located at Kings Point, NY, exists to serve the national interest that is inherent in America's commercially based, logistical sea power. Established in 1943, it is under the Maritime Administration, an agency within the Department of Transportation. The academy offers a four-year undergraduate program which leads to a Bachelor of Science degree, a U.S. Coast Guard license as a Third Mate or Third Assistant Engineer, and a commission as an Ensign in the U.S. Navy Reserve.

The academy is accredited by the Middle States Association of Colleges and Schools and both the Marine Engineering Systems and Marine Engineering & Shipyard Management curricula are accredited by the Accreditation Board for Engineering and Technology (ABET), 111 Market Place, Suite 1050, Baltimore MD 21202-4012, telephone: (410) 347-7700.

Student Life

Military life at the United States Merchant Marine Academy is a vital part of the total educational experience, and all midshipmen are required to meet high standards of conduct and discipline. The student body is organized along military lines as a regiment, under command of the senior class, and the military program is carefully designed to develop leadership ability, self-discipline and a sense of responsibility.

While the academic program is a demanding one, there is also ample time to participate in a wide variety of extracurricular activities. In addition to varsity athletics in 26 intercollegiate sports, a wide variety of club sports and intramurals permits all students to enjoy physical activity and competition. Student publications and the Radio Club, Camera Club, Regimental Band and Chess Club are a few of the special interest groups on campus. The Band, with a national reputation for excellence, plays for morning colors and at parades and performs in concert. The Band also has performed in presidential inaugural parades, at the Cotton Bowl in Dallas, Texas, for the National Horse Show in New York, the opening of the D-Day Museum in New Orleans, the Changing of the Guard at the Citadel in Quebec City, Canada (the only non-Canadian band afforded that honor), and in the Macy's Thanksgiving Day Parade. Under the guidance of a professional sailing master, the Kings Point Sailing Squadron offers midshipmen an opportunity to participate in top competitive intercollegiate and ocean racing, as well as gain experience in small and large boat handling and develop a "sea sense." The academy hosts the two largest intercollegiate regattas in the nation, the Nevins Trophy and the Admiral's Cup. Kings Point's sailing team currently ranks as one of the best in the nation.

For those interested in arts and world affairs, a stimulating series of lectures and concerts is provided on campus, and the academy's proximity to New York City (20 miles to mid-town Manhattan) places rock concerts, symphonies, Broadway shows, professional sports, museums, opera and ballet within easy reach.

Midshipmen are granted liberty on weekends, a fall break in early November, leave periods during Thanksgiving and the winter holidays in December, and a spring break in March, as well as annual leave during the month of July.

Enrollment
990 men and women.

Officer Programs

The USMMA is the largest source of U.S. Navy Reserve officers for the Merchant Marine Reserve/Navy Reserve. Each candidate must meet physical, moral and other requirements to become a Navy Reserve midshipman. He or she must apply for and accept a Reserve officer commission in the Navy or other branch of the armed services. Graduates are subject to a statutory obligation that requires the maintenance of the Navy Reserve status for eight years.

Admission Requirements

A candidate must be an American citizen and should be at least 17, but not have attained 25 years of age as of 1 July of the year of entry. Candidates must be nominated by a Member of Congress and compete for vacancies allocated to their State in proportion to its representation in Congress. A candidate's competitive standing is determined by his or her high school academic record, rank in class, SAT Reasoning Test or ACT standardized test scores, recommendations, leadership development potential, interest in the maritime industry, and the potential to develop into a competent Merchant Marine and Navy Reserve officer. Required tests must be taken within 18 months of the application deadline.

Minimum Requirements

1. All candidates must have completed the following: four years of English, three years of mathematics, to include Algebra I and II, Geometry and Trigonometry or Pre-Calculus; and one year of either laboratory Chemistry or Physics.

2. To be considered minimally qualified, a candidate must meet the following criteria:

ACT:	English	24
	Mathematics	24
Composite ACT: a least 23		
SAT-I:	Critical Reading/Verbal	560
	Mathematics	560

Combined SAT: at least 1120

3. Class Rank: Candidates should be in the top 40 percent of their Class or have compensating (better than mean) SAT Reasoning Test or ACT test scores and above-average math and science grades to be considered minimally qualified.

Shipboard Training Program

All midshipmen participate in this unique training program whereby they are assigned, during three (3) of the six (6) Trimesters of their sophomore and junior years, to commercially operated American-flag merchant ships. While aboard ship, in addition to shipboard duties, midshipmen are required to complete special written assignments ("sea projects") in a wide variety of professional subjects. This unique program takes them to many parts of the world (usually 15 to 18 different countries) and provides them with practical experience on several different types of ships. During the combined ten months of travel aboard ships, their campus is the Seven Seas. Midshipmen are paid a monthly stipend from the shipping companies they are assigned to, while sailing on board their ships.

Service Obligation

All midshipmen, in return for their attending the academy's four-year program at taxpayer expense, must serve five years in the maritime industry or on active duty as an officer in the U.S. Navy or another branch of the uniformed services. Commissions may be obtained in the U.S. Army, U.S. Marine Corps, U.S. Navy, U.S. Air Force or U.S. Coast Guard. Service as an officer on active duty in the National Oceanic and Atmospheric Administration (NOAA) is also acceptable. If graduates choose the maritime industry, they have a military Reserve obligation of eight years. Graduates must also maintain a current (valid) license as either a Third Mate or Third Assistant Engineer (or higher) for six years after graduation.

Careers

Graduates of the Academy seek employment as licensed ship's officers on American-flag merchant vessels. It should be noted, however, that employment in the maritime industry is cyclical along with the nation's economy, and seagoing jobs are at times not readily available. At those times, the Secretary of Transportation, based on recommendations of the Maritime Administrator, may authorize shore-side employment in maritime and transportation-related industries.

Many graduates, after fulfilling their obligations, attain leadership positions in the maritime industry. Some areas in which they are typically employed include: canal, river, and harbor pilots; cargo broker; dredging; inter-modal transportation; marine engineering; maritime insurance; maritime labor; marine surveyor; maritime training; admiralty law; nuclear propulsion' oceanography; offshore drilling; shipbuilding and repair; ship chartering; steamship company management; stevedoring and terminal operations; towing and barging; and naval architecture.

Nominations

Candidates must be nominated by a Member of Congress. The two U.S. Senators and each U.S. Representative, including each U.S. Delegate to the House of Representatives from Guam, the Virgin Islands, the District of Columbia, and American Samoa as well as the Resident Commissioner from the Commonwealth of Puerto Rico, may each annually nominate ten candidates for the academy. Members of the House of Representatives may nominate anyone within their state to the Academy (this differs from nominations to the DoD academies, where they are limited to nominating only those who reside within their district). Congressional nominations can now be submitted online. The USMMA will be mailing out instructions on how to get into the Congressional portal. If you have any questions, please contact Ms. Jamie Quick at (516) 726-5646 or email quickj@usmma.edu. Nominations .should be submitted no later than 31 January (31 December if the Member is not returning to office in the next session of Congress). Candidates should be encouraged to return their completed application to the academy as early as possible. The deadline for application submission is 1 March.

Cost and Financial Aid

There is no tuition or room/board charged to USMMA students. In addition, the government covers the cost of their uniforms and books. However, other normal expenses (purchase of laptop at the outset of their first (freshman) year, activity and service fees, etc.) are the responsibility of the students.

Midshipmen at the academy are not paid a monthly stipend as cadets/midshipmen are at the DoD and DHS academies. The only time they are paid is during the shipboard training period (called "Sea Year"), as described earlier.

To help financially-needy or economically-disadvantaged students meet their other normal expenses, the academy participates in several federal financial aid programs sponsored by the U.S. Education Department. Loans available to USMMA midshipmen to include student Stafford loans (subsidized and unsubsidized) and parent PLUS loans. Grants available include, PELL. In addition, those students eligible to receive "outside" scholarships are encouraged to apply for them, as those can be used to satisfy their billed expenses. A small number of scholarships donated to the academy by outside organizations are also used to assist those midshipmen who have the greatest need, and who meet whatever other criteria may be set by the donor organization.

Important Phone Numbers

Admissions Office	(516) 773-5391
Toll-free	(866) 546-4778
Fax	(516) 773-5390

Website: www.usmma.edu
E-mail address: admission@usmma.edu

Financial Aid Office	(516) 726-5638

E-mail address: financialaid@usmma.edu

SECTION 4

Department of Defense Medical Examination Review Board (DODMERB)

Department of Defense Medical Examination Review Board (DODMERB)

Congressional **Staff** questions may be submitted to the Deputy Director, DODMERB, 24 hours a day, 7 days a week all year long at the following email address. Lawrence.E.Mullen.civ@mail.mil

The Department of Defense Medical Examination Review Board (DODMERB) is responsible for determining if applicants meet medical accession standards for all US Service Academies, Reserve Officer Training Corps (ROTC) programs, and the Uniformed Services University of the Health Sciences (USUHS). DODMERB or a civilian contractor (currently Concorde Inc., Philadelphia, PA) will contact applicants to schedule these medical examination appointments. The government will pay for a complete medical and optometric examination. Many applicants apply to more than one Academy and some Reserve Officer Training Programs (ROTC). Regardless of the number of Academies and/or ROTC programs applied to, the applicant will only be required to obtain one examination.

After the applicant has completed a medical and optometric (eye) examination, DODMERB will inform the applicants and the Academy(ies) of the medical status. If there is a need for additional medical tests, and/or evaluations, and/or information, DODMERB will send the applicant a letter requesting these, otherwise known as *remedials*. Applicants may visit https://dodmerb.tricare.osd.mil to access information about DODMERB and then go to "Frequently Asked Questions" (option tab "FAQs"), or to track their medical status. Click on option tab "Applicant." This is their primary source of obtaining information from DODMERB.

Applicants must bring photo identification to their examination. If the applicant is under eighteen years of age, they should contact the examining facility to see if there is a requirement for a parent or guardian to accompany them to the examination.

Applicants accepting offers of appointment to a US Service Academy will undergo HIV and drug/alcohol-abuse testing as required by Public Law (Title 10, US Code, Section 978) within 72 hours of arrival at an Academy.

Applicant questions concerning their medical status or examination scheduling may be emailed to usaf.usafa.dodmerb.mbx.helpdesk@mail.mil or via letter to DODMERB, 8034 Edgerton Drive, Suite 132, USAF Academy, CO 80840-2200 (please include a daytime phone number and/or e-mail address).

DODMERB compares the results of the completed medical examination, the completed medical history, (and any other documentation submitted as a remedial) TO the medical accession standards listed in the Department of Defense Instruction 6130.4, Medical Accession Standards for Appointment, Enlistment and Induction at (http://www.dtic.mil/whs/directives/corres/pdf/613004p.pdf).

This results in one of two determinations:

Determination 1 – __MEETS__ medical accession standards
Determination 2 – __DOES NOT__ meet medical accession standards

All applicants who do not meet medical accession standards will be automatically reviewed by each Academy Admissions office to which the applicant has applied. The applicant is NOT required to take any action. If the Admissions office feels the applicant has the potential to receive an appointment, they will direct their assigned medical waiver authority to consider a medical waiver.

This will result in one of three decisions:

Decision 1 - Medical waiver granted
Decision 2 - Medical waiver denied
Decision 3 - The medical waiver authority may request remedials to consider before they render their final waiver decision of granted or denied.